PENIS CIRCUS

THIS FUNNY BOOK FOR THE MAN'S LITTLE FRIEND CONTAINS 19 DIFFERENT PICTURES.

YOU CAN CUT THEM TO YOUR INDIVIDUAL SIZE.

IT IS ALSO GREAT AS A FUN FINGER GAME.

HAVE FUN!

INSTRUCTIONS

1.CHOOSE YOUR DESIRED MOTIF

2.CUT OUT THE APPROPRIATE SIZE ALONG THE DOTTED LINE

3.PUT YOUR DESIRED BODY PART THROUGH AND DISCOVER THE CIRCUS WORLD

CONTACT: ANNEMEYER235@GMAIL.COM